THE STORY OF OLD SEACOMBE

P. Davies

CONTENTS

Title Page
Introduction ... 1
Seacombe Village ... 3
In And Around Seacombe ... 4
Those Early Days of the Ferry ... 7
Living In Squalor ... 12
Seacombe Well ... 16
Railway At Seacombe ... 21
Looking at old Seacombe ... 24
Seacombe Industry ... 29
A Look Around Seacombe: Pictorial ... 33
Concertina Cottages ... 45
Seacombe Shipyards ... 52
Looking at Old Victoria Road ... 54
The Irving Theatre ... 58
A Decade of Change ... 61
Acknowledgements ... 69

INTRODUCTION

Seacombe Ferry, 1815
*****

Seacombe has always loomed largely in the early records of our Borough, though owing to alterations to the contour of the River, arising from natural, and partly from artificial causes, this part of the Borough is now very different from that which existed in the earlier days.

Mrs. Hannah Fisher wrote in a book of verse about Seacombe which was published in Australia in 1889:

"Lanes of Seacombe, green and leafy,
Scenes no more that bless my sight.

Where no scent of hawthorne lingered
On the zephyr's wing at night".

The lanes were described as green and leafy, and with a lingering scent of hawthorne. That was how a poet sang of old Seacombe. And that was just as it was. This was a time before the tower blocks of flats and rows of maisonettes, before the road widening, and the changes that town planners brought about. The south end of town was very much the village. Right up to the 1920s it kept about it a character all its own. Now it has changed again from a mainly shopping area to a residential area. Just a place like any other place. The character has long disappeared.

SEACOMBE VILLAGE

Seacombe is derived from "Cwm", a cup shaped hollow by the sea. The Cheshire word for a brewing vat is "combe" or "coom". There was a Seccum Village mentioned in the Doomsday Book, although it is suggested by some historians that this passage referred more specifically to the Ferry service which was maintained across the old Wallasey Pool, which is now the Wallasey and Birkenhead docks, rather than to the passage between Seacombe and Liverpool. There is also a mention of Seccum in 1354, when a Samson family were the big local landowners.

The Seacombe Village in the early nineteenth century consisted of just a few houses. There is no concrete evidence available of the original site of Seacombe Village and Ferry but there is mention of ferries across the Pool, and the name Seacombe render it quite possible that the settlement and the ferry were situated near the head of the numerous creeks which branched from Wallasey Pool between Poulton and the Mersey.

Lands in Seacombe passed into various hands over the years. By the 1800s the area had become a place of substance. In 1850 it was described as a country village. It had 'lanes and leafy bowers'. There is evidence that in the 1500s and 1600s there was a herring curing industry here.

IN AND AROUND SEACOMBE

West Seacombe Terrace (now Percy Road) had large houses occupied by the rather well-to-do. ship owners and merchants from Liverpool had their homes there. Every house had its servants quarters. There were entrances for tradesmen.

At 53 Demesne Street was Seacombe Cottage Hospital. Further along was the Abbotsford Hotel. Off Brighton Street was the Vienna Hall (later the Marina Cinema). It was built by a Mr. Emmanuel Kopetzki, who came from the Austrian city.

Up to 100 years ago there was a clear view of Bidston Hill from the terrace. It was a walk from there to Oakdale, the Dock Road, and a path across the marsh to Bidston.

Westland House, at the top of the terrace, became the vicarage for St. Paul's Church, built in 1846, with its 120 foot high spire a local landmark.

Guinea Gap Baths (above) was opened on April 7th, 1908 at the cost of £25,000. Water is pumped from the River Mersey. It was not until 19?5 that mixed bathing was permitted – though that was only allowed on Saturday evenings. The first manager of the baths was Mr. J. Finlay, who interestingly was the first bather of the New Brighton Opening Air Pool.

Opposite the baths on River View Road was Seacombe Laundry. The business began in a small house in Borough Road in the 1880's before opening in River View Road in 1909.

The postal service began in Wallasey in 1866. There were four Post Offices. One was at 79 Albion Street, one at 144 Wallasey Road; another at 171 Wallasey Village and one was located at 26 Brighton Street. In those early years letters were delivered from Birkenhead Post. Office until about 1892, when a sorting and delivery office was opened in Liscard Village. Two postmen had to trudge over from Birkenhead and deliver the letters to Seacombe and Dock Road.

Riverview Road, Seacombe Steam Laundry dry cleaning, 1963

Old Seacombe began to break up just after World War One. Courts and alleys vanished in clouds of brick dust in the 1920s and 1930s.

The blitzes of World War Two brought toppling down most of what the demolition men and the clearance orders missed.

The cobbles have gone, and the quaint old corners, and 'Piggy Jone's Field'.

Gone are the little cottages with the big gardens. Gone are the horses and carts. 'The Blocks', and Mersey Street.

THOSE EARLY DAYS OF THE FERRY

There was a ferry – of sorts – as long as the fifteenth century. Between about 1635 and 1775 the ferry was mainly used to bring people over from Liverpool to go and watch the horse racing which ran between Wallasey Village across the sand dunes to Leasowe Castle and back.

In 1761 John Wilson sold his Seacombe boats to John Owen who, ten years later, sold them, plus land, to Rear-Admiral Richard Smith. Upon his death in 1811, his son, Richard Smith, inherited the ferry.

By the begining of the 19th Century no attempt was ever made to provide any fixed landing on the Wallasey side of the Mersey. It was Richard Smith who completed a new earth and store slipway in about 1815. He was the Lord of the Manor of Poulton-cum-Seacombe and owned much of the land in Seacombe and Poulton.

Local Trustees financed the slipway and were very anxious to lease the site. The first lessee was believed to be the owner of the newly built Stanley Hotel. Stanley Garner. The Stanley Hotel was situated in Borough Road.

New hotels started to pop up along the Wirral coast and one of these enterprising gentlemen was Mr. Thomas Parry who built the original Seacombe Ferry Hotel in 1819. The two-story building had gardens, a bowling green, a summer house and even an American-style bowling alley.

Seacombe Ferry, 1830

In the same year the Seacombe Ferry Hotel was opened Mr. Parry acquired the ferry lease from Richard Smith. He improved the slipway, and eventually a jetty with an extension which could be launched into the river to deal with the varying tidal levels, was constructed. The structure was in use until 1876.

The early means of ferrying passengers was by small boats which were either single or double-masted but they were slow and irregular – also dependant on the weather. However, in 1829, steams boats were plying every hour from Liverpool.

By the 1850's Mr. Parry decided to sell the hotel to John Stokes. The large hotel was renamed Stokes Seacombe Hotel for a time. Eliza Stokes became the owner in 1877 and she was to oversee a new hotel being built on reclaimed land a year later.

Seacombe Ferry, 1840

Seacombe Ferry, c1850. Seacombe Ferry Hotel left centre. Marine Hotel extreme left.

In 1861 the old Wallasey Local Board took control of the ferry stations at New Brighton, Egremont and Seacombe from two brothers, Edward and William Coulborn, who had been the owners since 1854. Mr. Braithwaite Pool was the first Ferry Manager. His first job was to improve the service. One of the first changes was to introduce a bye-law which banned passengers from singing and the playing of musical instruments. Hawkers and pedlars were also banned from ferry premises which caused some protests from the public in particular the barring of an old woman who had sold oranges and gingerbread at Seacombe.

View of Seacombe Ferry, 1876

Ferry passengers, who were quite often brought over on a fishing boat, had to run down the stage to escape the water splashing them between the planks. They paid the ticket collector whilst he had waves lashing round his legs and feet at the turnstiles. He had a little box, like a watch man's hut. Later a gangway was added for passengers to disembark but many people tended to jump on and off the ferryboats. This unfortunately caused accidents, as people frequently fell into the river. The Local Board decided to put a stop to this jumping off and engaged half a dozen police officers to travel on the boats and take names of the offenders. On the first day a number of names and addresses were taken and summonses issued but when they came to court the Magistrates' Clerk asked what bye-law the Board was acting. As there was no bye-law, the prosecution failed and the summonses were withdrawn. The Local Board, finding the officers were useless, asked the Chief Constable to withdraw his men, but he refused as he had engaged other men to take their place. The result was that the policeman had to travel on the boats with nothing to do but smoke and play cards.

Seacombe Ferry, 1880

It became evident by 1875 that this state of affairs could not continue, and in 1877 the land which the high tide ran along the line of Birkenhead Road was filled in. A wall was thrown across the front, making a straight line, in which the stage and bridge was placed and the new Ferry hotel and shops built. During these operations a temporary stage was erected on the wall of the ship-building yard at East Street. The total cost of the development which included a new terminal, a hydraulic lift and tower in connection with the luggage-boat service and gangways was £143,000 (about £7 million in today's money).

LIVING IN SQUALOR

One of the most important milestones in the development of the Wirral, especially for Wallasey was the reduction of ferry fares in 1848. The cost of the fare was 2d but this was reduced to 1d. Instead of a weekly fare of two shillings it was now just one shilling. In those days a shilling bought a working-class family a lot of food. It resulted in a greater mobility of labour – many families wanting to escape the squalor of Liverpool began to settle in the new properties now being built in Wallasey.

However, the sudden influx of hundreds of families into Seacombe's tiny community caused the construction of many abominable hovels which had no running water or sanitation. The poorest houses were in Mersey Street. Many people lived in the dark, overcrowded and damp cellars. The houses were all swept away under a demolition order about 1930. Nor far away, close to Demesne Street, was a court known locally as Little Hell. The houses here were poor and dilapidated and by the 1900's were demolished by the old Wallasey Urban District Council.

The provision of health care throughout Wallasey was very poor in the 19th century. The earliest medical care was the Wallasey Dispensary, which was a charitable outpatient service for the poor, started in 1831 in Littler's Terrace, row of houses situated between Church Street and the old King's Arms pub, it was later sited in Demesne Street.

Another medical centre was the Seacombe Dispensary for Children which was started in 1867 by a single benefactor, Mr. E.G. Hammond, and was in Fell Street.

Mersey Street, 1908.

In 1871 it combined with the Seacombe Cottage Hospital which had opened (as part of the Wallasey Dispensary) in January 1867 and moved to new premises in Demesne Street. All three institutions combined and became known as the 'Wallasey and Seacombe Cottage Hospitals and Wallasey Dispensary' and remained so until 1901 when they were all replaced by the Victoria Central Hospital which opened in 1901 in Liscard Road.

Oakdale Court, 1908

For much of the century only the Wallasey Dispensary was available for the poor. There were private doctors for those who could afford them. The president of the charity was John Penkett and they were funded by local donations to provide medicines and consultations to the poor. A working-man could pay 6 shillings (30p) per annum, which entitled medical care for him and his family.

There was a major problem with effective sewage and drainage in Seacombe (as well as Poulton). The drains and sewers from the properties deposited on the Seacombe shore. The stench was bad but the diseases it carried were harmful to health. Quite often cesspools were used for the disposal of excrement which the Night Soilmen had to empty. A very unpleasant task. Their job was to shovel up the muck into carts and remove and deposit it elsewhere in the Parish. As the population grew the cesspools contaminated the nearby wells causing many people to become ill. There was some form of local government in Wallasey called the Wallasey Commissioners who worked chiefly through a 'Wallasey Improvement Committee'. Their task was to deal with health water supply, drainage and sewers but they were largely ineffectual and though they were meant to investigate any "nuisances" they concentrated on road improvements and minor complaints such as the smell of a pigsty in Mersey Street.

The sewerage issue became worse when in early 1846 the Birkenhead Docks Commissioners carried out excavation work in the Wallasey Pool and had blocked up the main sewer. The clerk of the Improvement Committee was instructed to write to the Birkenhead Docks Commissioners about the problem but nothing was resolved. The Docks Commissioners had, since 1844, been constructing the new docks in the Wallasey Pool but by August 1847 they went bankrupt, throwing many Seacombe men out of work. Only two small docks were completed but with Government financial assistance the work began again in March 1849. A temporary dam across the Pool was constructed on the east side of the Great Float which led to sewage accumulation on the Seacombe shore, resulting in a cholera outbreak in the Parish. Several inhabitants perished.

The response of the Improvement Committee was to put up notices instructing the locals to white-wash their homes, and to "remove all filth and noxious matter which may be found deposited or accumulated in any of the public highways or private streets".

This was not good enough and something more had to be done and so in 1851 a considerable number of inhabitants of Seacombe petitioned the General Board of Health to act. After a report by the Superintendent Inspector, Robert Rawlinson, it was found that Seacombe had no public lights, limited gasworks, no public supply of water, and the roads were dirty, especially in the winter. It was also found that the infant mortality rate was worse than that of Liverpool.

There were some improvements in sanitary conditions but overall little was done by the newly formed Wallasey Local Board and cholera was to return to Seacombe two further times and take more lives. It cannot be by coincidence that once the Wallasey Docks were completed in 1865 Cholera never returned.

SEACOMBE WELL

The Clock Tower at the corner of Borough Road and Church Road, Seacombe, until the 1930's. was at one time the offices of the 'Wallasey News,' which marked the spot the site of the old Village Pump of Seacombe. In 1900 a newspaper and stationer's shop stood on this spot and adjoining it was the 'Five Bars Rest' (where the Village band of those days had their headquarters). The property belonged to Mr. Thomas Montgomery and he secured the newspaper shop adjoining in 1900, in order to extend his premises under an agreement with the District Council by which he set back the Victoria Road (as the road was called then) frontage several feet. The extension marked the site of the old Village pump.

Somewhere in the early years of the 19th Century, long before Wallasey had any organised form of government, a well was sunk here, surrounded by a small wall, and the villagers visited it at various times of the day to fetch water required for domestic consumption.

Mr. E. Kopetzky who came to Seacombe in 1859 and who was a tenant of the second storey of the corner premises demolished in 1900, left behind him one or two records which are of interest. He stated that his wife's mother – Mrs. Little, a member, by the way, of an old Seacombe family, from which Little Street, off Brighton Street, took its name – told him that twenty years previous to his coming (1839) she was in the habit of going to the well for water. The water, however became brackish and the well was ultimately disused and filled up. In 1900 the circular wall was demolished and the only trace that remained was the old brick work found in the cellar in the clock tower.

Demesne Street

The pump was worked by a handle similar to that of an old wringing machine, which had been in use since 1848. The pump was open to the public generally, but the water was very brackish, especially when the tide was up, and most people preferred to use better water from the well on the premises of Mr. Leicester, butcher, at that time on Borough Road, or from Farmer Evans in Church Road.

Mr. Kopetzky's account of Seacombe in the 1860's makes an interesting story, in view of the many changes that took place over the following decades. The great trouble at that seemed to be to obtain water fit to drink. The village pump water became so brackish that housewives had even for washing to rely on water from a pit in Brougham Road. It was a common thing to see on washing-day (Monday) a long string of cans being borne by the sturdy housewives of Seacombe or other members of the family from this pond.

The proprietor of the Seacombe Hotel (which stood considerably back from the old Seacombe Hotel) had a large waterbutt, drawn by a horse, constructed for the purpose of conveying water to his establishment.

Another way in which many of the Seacombe people were supplied at that period was by means of cisterns and wells, placed underneath the kitchen floor. The rain water was conducted from the roofs of their houses into these wells and then was pumped up to the sink-stone as required. Some of these disused wells were uncovered when the old properties in Demense Street were demolished in the 1920s. They were in some instances found directly underneath the kitchens in which the families had lived and must have formed a constant source of danger to health and life.

The Wallasey News building, corner of Church Street, 1924

In one house Edward Parkinson, who demolished the property, found a wringing machine down of the receptacles. Mr. Kopetzky related that in his time in the house in which he was living the flag covering fell in and a girl went down into the hole and narrowly escaped with her life.

The house occupied by Mr. Kopetzky in the 1860s was at the corner of Chapel Street – then described as "The end of Seacombe". That was to say there was no property between there and Beaufort Terrace (where the Town Hall South Annexe office is today on Brighton Street). The other side of the road, from Brighton Place northwards, was occupied by a considerable distance of brickfields and allotment gardens.

Seacombe Promenade decorated for Coronation Day, June 1911

It is interesting to notice that at this early period, though Seacombe householders were destitute of many conveniences, they had a sort of public clock. This was placed in the spire of the then Wesleyan Chapel – which was situated at the opposite corner of Borough Road to the stationers shop, with a garden in front. The clock struck the hours, and the local tradesmen were in the habit of subscribing a shilling a year to keep it going.

On Birkenhead Road was The Marine Hotel which was also knows as 'Brassey's'. The pub was formerly two fisherman's cottages and dates back to the late eighteenth century and closed in 1992 to make way for road widening, Next door was an irregular row of whitewashed brick cottages. There were masses of flowers in their gardens.

One of the cottages was originally thatched and was kept as an eating house. This would seem to have been the original ferry-house at Seacombe when the high-tide at one time ran along Birkenhead Road.

RAILWAY AT SEACOMBE

Between 1840 and 1866 several new lines of railway was constructed on the Wirral. In 1866 the Wirral Railway was built from Birkenhead Docks Station to Hoylake. Wallasey however, was ignored until 1886, when, following upon the opening of the Mersey Tunnel Railway with its attention to Birkenhead Park station, a branch line of the Wirral Railway was constructed to New Brighton via Wallasey Village. Shortly afterwards, an additional branch line was extended to Seacombe Ferry from which station a railway was constructed in the years 1888-1895 running through Bidston, Heswall, and across the centre of the Wirral via Heswall Hills, Neston, Connah's Quay and Shelton to North

Wales. change at Birkenhead Park from steam to electric trains has always militated against the success of this line,

View of the properties that were demolished to make way for Seacombe station, c1875

The station was opened on 1st June 1895 and replaced old properties that once stood on thr site. The station was originally only intended as temporary. The frontage of the station was made of corrugated iron. It was intended to extend the line a further 140 yards where the ferry terminal and railway were to br built adjacent to each other. The plan was never carried out. In fact the station platform was always dimly lit at night, only source of illumination came from gas lamps.

On 3rd January 1960 the Seacombe line was closed to passengers and three years later it ceased to carry goods. The line lay direlct for many years, until plans for s second Mersey Tunnel were passed. The actual rail line was used to link the new tunnel, opened in 1971, with the new M53 motorway.

THE STORY OF OLD SEACOMBE

An LMS design 2-6-T at Seacombe Station. In the background is the clock tower of Seacombe Ferry Terminal.

LOOKING AT OLD SEACOMBE

19th Century view of Birkenheaad Road leading to Seacombe Ferry Entrance - shipyards on the right

---

Seacombe at the turn of the 20th Century was already built up with terraces of little houses and many roads and small streets. Pavements in the old days were narrow. There were no noises from the traffic roar of modern engines.

Over a century ago the tram cars rattled through a Seacombe of lively streets, gaslight that hissed at night, giving off a mustard yellow glow. It may not have been the richest part of town but it was bursting with life. There were the calls of the coalmen, the old clothesmen, of hawkers' cries and of rumbling cart wheels. Old Seacombe had character and colour.

Bank House, 1904.

Situated close to the Seacombe Hotel, on the corner of Borough Road and Mersey Street. Bank House was originally known as 'Green Bank' in the 1870s and the occupier was a wine and spirit merchant, John Andrews. A multi-storey block of flats, Mersey Court, now occupy the site. Before the area was built up there was then one main street Victoria (now Borough) Road, two or three cross streets, a terrace or two scattered houses and some small industries.

In Smithy Lane, once off Borough Road, there was the sound of hammer hitting anvil in the busy blacksmith's shop. There was the Mersey Street area. Not far away, close to Demesne Street, was a court known as Little Hell. Set in the walls of most small streets were middens – communal dustbins emptied by horse drawn wagons. Hop-scotch played on the pavements. Street singers and Spanish onion men.

If it were possible to take a stroll round the area as it was 120 or 130 years ago you would stumble on much that would enterprise.

You would find Catherine Terrace, in Ferryview Road. It was considered a rather special place. It consisted of three houses built in the 1820s. Surrounding them was the poor tightly-packed property known as Mersey Street area. It was all swept away under a demolition order about 1930.

Ferry View Road, `c1912.

Near the Seacombe end of Birkenhead Road was a gateway with the words 'Marine Parade' over it, carved on a painted board. This stood until the early 1920s.

Adjoining the Marine Hotel (better known later as 'Brassey's pub) which stood on Birkenhead Road there was up to about 120 years ago an irregular row of whitewashed brick cottages. There were masses of flowers in the gardens. The oldest of the cottages was originally thatched and kept as an eating house by one Daniel Torney. This would seem to have been the original ferry house at Seacombe.

Seacombe Police Station (pictured above) once stood opposite where the Liver View Hotel is today and opened in 1904 in Church Road. The two storey building was built of red brick with two entrances. There was a lockup prison cell and living quarters for a permanent Police Officer in residence. The station would serve the local community for more than 60 years.Belle Vue Road and all between that and what is now Borough Road was occupied by Belle Vue Tea and Pleasure Gardens.

Oakdale Road was a dale. North from the top of Borough Road fields stretched away towards Liscard.

All the land from the top of Borough Road to Mill Lane was farm land belonging to the Mainwaring family of Shropshire and Denbighshire, from whom Mainwaring Road gets its name. Gorsedale Road was known as Cinder Lane, with green fields sloping down to Wallasey Pool.

Running up from the Dock Road near Gorsey Lane was Creek Side, a name which recalled that Wallasey Pool was not always confined between dock walls.

Wheatland House, 1912, An old thatched cottage built in 1864 and located on Wheatland Lane, next to the Bee Hotel (later O'Sheas, now a convenience store). Philip Wilson once lived at the house and he married the daughter of Thomas Meols of Wallasey Hall.

Some of the old roads in Seacombe derive their names from local historical or geographical connections. Builders would also adopt the practice of giving street names to blocks of buildings. Beaconsfield Road, which once ran off Demesne Street, was named after Lord Beaconsfield, Beatrice Street after Princess Beatrice, Leopold Street after Prince Leopold and Gladstone Road after Prime Minister William Gladstone.

SEACOMBE INDUSTRY

Seacombe had its industries. It had mills and factories. There was the Seacombe Pottery which opened in 1852 with six large kilns down by the docks, off Wheatland Lane. The kilns produced earthenware and stoneware which were beautifully colour-printed of purple or blue tint.

The founder of the pottery industry was John Goodwin who came to Seacombe from Staffordshire. The locals called John the 'Potter of Seacombe'. It was the first of the industries to come to Seacombe. There was awful poverty and hungry children in the area so Goodwin's pottery brought work to local families. John's son, Thomas Orton Goodwin, carried on the business after his father's death in 1857. He resided at 148 Wheatland Lane. Unfortunately, in the same year, misfortune was to hit the business when an uninsured consignment of the goods was lost at sea on the way to the Americas. It resulted in a financial embarrassment and production was ceased.

Though the pottery business was short lived I think, however, that the Goodwin's place in the story of the parish has been underestimated. The family certainly played an important part in the development of Seacombe in the mid-19th Century.

There were other businesses in Seacombe. There was the sugar refinery which was managed by John Horbury who lived at West Seacombe Terrace (Percy Road) in the 1860's.

There was also Mawdsley and Smith's Smalt Works, which stood on the Dock Road near the junction with Birkenhead Road. Mr. Mawdsley resided in Pool Cottage which was near his works but was demolished once the Great Float was completed in 1860.

View of Seacombe Pottery, 1889

In Havelock Street was the Phospho Peruvian Guano Works which commence about 1830. The local residents had to endure the odour.

Currie Rowlands, the fertilizer manufacturers, commenced in Seacombe in 1894 on the former grounds on the Seacombe Pottery. Bibby, Sons and Company's Copper Works stood near Creek Side off the Dock Road and was founded in 1812. Mr. Roberts was the manager until it closed in about 1863. He lived in Creek House which was nearby. Some of the cottages occupied by the workmen remained until 1959.

Just north of the Copper Works was the cement works which had been established in 1855 by George F. Chantrell who came from Leeds. Just nearby stood the old Vitriol Works of Clough and Galan.

Gandy Belt opened in Wheatland Lane in 1895 by Captain Maurice Gandy. He set up his business in Wapping, Liverpool some sixteen years earlier but decided to move the factory to Seacombe. He began his earlier life as a seafarer but after being shipwrecked he decided to retire and became a ship-owner and cloth manufacturer in 1865. However, not happy with the venture, Captain Gandy longed to start something new. His Gandy Belts works had branches all over the world. There was an unfortunate serious fire at the works on 18th February, 1927. The fire caused £250,000 in damages. The fire alarm in the works was raised at 3.50pm.

There were normally about 300 men and women employed, but owing to slackness in trade, a proportion was on short time. Consequently, the building, which was well equipped with fire exits, was quickly cleared.

Within less than half an hour of the alarm being sounded the fire had swept through the middle of the building and flames were of a terrific height.

The fire spread outwards to each wing. The occupants of the houses on the left hand side of Vernon Avenue watched the progress of the flames with anxiety. There was no space or entry between the backs of these houses and the works. The flames roared with intensity a few yards from them. The building nearest the avenue collapsed. The situation was so dangerous that families had to evacuate their homes and some even removed some of their belongings into the street – including their pianos.

In front of the works, in Wheatland Lane, a great crowd had gathered to watch in awe. However, the road was narrow between St. Paul's Road and Wheatland Lane junction, the heat rapidly became unbearable, and the onlookers had to leave.

It was with great effort by the fireman that the flames never took hold of the houses on Vernon Avenue. It was from the rear of the works that the full fury of the blaze could best be viewed. The flames leapt up in the air and huge clouds of black oil smoke belched forth. The fire continued long after nightfall and the flames could be seen as far away as Great Orme's Head. The cause of the outbreak of the fire was believed to be caused by fusing of a wire. The works was full of highly flammable materials which were the main cause of the fire spreading rapidly. The factory fire put many local people out of work and it was many months before the factory was re-built and modernised. By the 1980s the factory closed and moved to Birkenhead and so ending nearly a century of association with Seacombe.

A LOOK AROUND SEACOMBE: PICTORIAL

Looking In & Around old Seacombe

Victoria Place looking up Demesne Strett, 1952

Wheatland Lane junction with Kelvin Road 16.6.1954

Wheatland Lane junction with Palermo Street, 16.06.1954

Palermo Street From Wheatland Lane, 16.06.1954

Palermo Street junction with Whetland Lane, 16.06.1954

THE STORY OF OLD SEACOMBE

Birkenhead Road looking towards Seacombe Ferry, 7.11.52

39

P. DAVIES

Oakdale Road, 14.04.1967

THE STORY OF OLD SEACOMBE

Smithy Lane with Borough Road in the distance, 13.06.1945

Municipal Wash House, Oakdale Road. Mayor opening, 03 1931

THE STORY OF OLD SEACOMBE

Oakdale Road viewed from the old railway bridge, 1954

Guinea Gap Baths interior, 1934

CONCERTINA COTTAGES

The following article is from a Municipal Engineering report, October 29th, 1954.

Wallasey has just completed the clearance, by clearance order, of 33 houses with a form of construction so unusual as to be unique in the experience of those who have seen them. It is said that there is nothing new under the sun, and perhaps somewhere there are or have been other houses of a similar pattern. If any reader has encountered the same kind of house construction and layout, the writer would be grateful for any information he would care to supply. This account of the design and condition of the houses in Wallasey - which exists no more - will not only serve as a permanent record of a form of construction which is not likely to be repeated, but will no doubt interest all those who in the next few years are to be engaged in the removal of unfit houses.

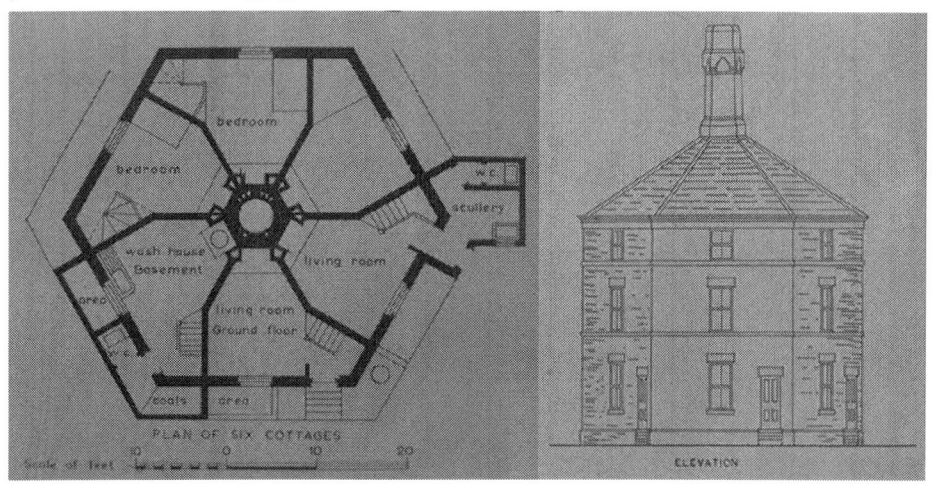

The 33 houses in the clearance area comprised six blocks. Five were hexagonal in plan, a shape which was responsible for their being popularity (but unofficially) known in the locality as "Concertina Cottages." A sixth block (block A on the sketch plan) consisted of three houses. One of the hexagonal blocks F and block A were joined to semi-detached houses, fronting the main road and of a traditional form of construction and layout, which were not included in the area.

It is possible that the four "front houses" may have been intended as dwellings for artisans or members of even a higher class, while the remainder are likely to have been built as labourers' cottages as understood in the nineteenth century.

The "concertina" cottages formed a miniature "estate" which was approached by an access road from the adjoining street. Each block was surrounded by a short depth of garden, the periphery of which followed the hexagonal outline of the blocks in plan. Between the garden fences were flagged approaches, with occasional trees situated for full decorative effect.

The open space between blocks, measured from and at right-angles to the main walls varied from 19ft. To 36ft. The hexagonal plan enabled certain houses to face the open space between the two adjoining blocks, and thus 11 of the 33 houses were overshadowed, and these only on the ground floor.

The internal layout of the houses, as conceived by the original builder and owner, is shown in the reproduction of his typical plan of 1874. It appears to have been his intention to cover a very large area with houses of similar design, since a block plan shows 29 groups of cottages, but for reasons not recorded, the project was not proceeded with. And though the deposited plan appears to have envisaged that all blocks would follow the same plan, no two blocks proved to be alike in all respects.

Nevertheless, the same principle applied to each of the blocks: each was to have only one external wall, this forming the front of the house.

The party walls between the houses converged radially towards the centre of each block, where there was a common chimney stack serving all houses. Thus, with few exceptions, all rooms were of unorthodox shape, with splayed walls and awkward corners, a factor which reduced the usefulness of the available floor space and provided an exercise in mensuration for the sanitary inspector doing the surveyor.

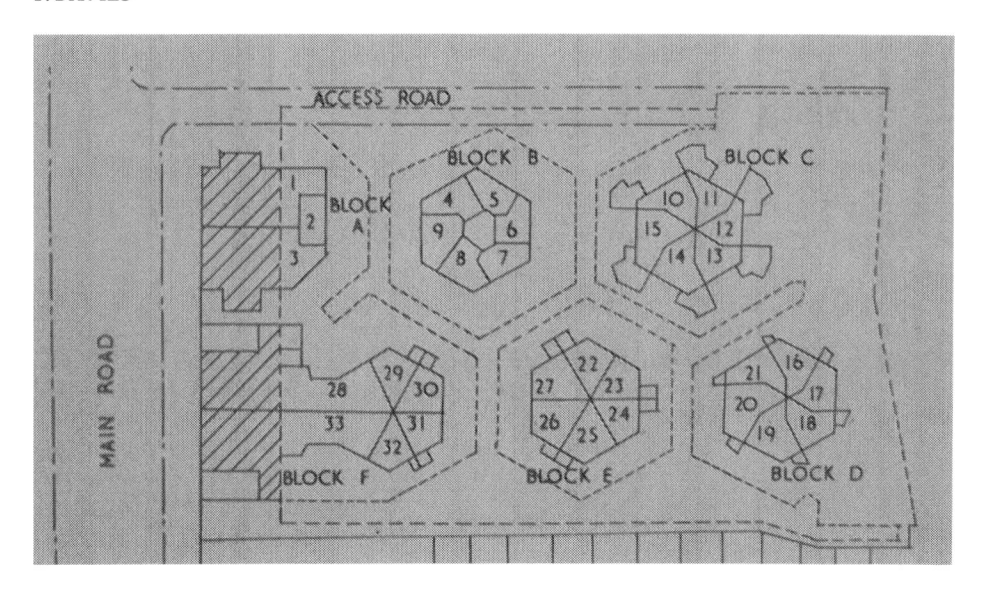

One Storey – one room

In blocks A, B, and C each storey contained only one room, bounded on each side by the house next door, and at the "rear" by the common chimney flue; from the theoretical point of view, it would be interesting to know whether the houses could be described as back-to-back!

In other matters of detail, each block – almost every house – was unlike its neighbour. Blocks A and B had basements and three storeys above ground. Block C, D and houses numbered 28 and 33 in block F were three-storeyed, without basements. The remaining houses in block F and blocks E had only tow storeys, and no basements.

The houses varied also in the attachments to the main structure. Those in blocks A and B had no additions to the main building, the front external doors opening into a small "hall" from which the stairs rose and into which the living room door opened. The yard was so restricted that it was possible to straddle across it with one foot on the threshold of the scullery, the other on the doorstep of the water closet apartment.

The additions to blocks D. E, F comprised open-air coal space and external water closet, in one case arranged singly, and in the other two, side-by-side. As an indication of the extent of the "yard space" in these blocks, the area inclusive of the water closet varied from 19 to 34 superficial feet.

Blocks A and B houses had no yard space. These were the blocks with basements, consisting of a single room which formed the scullery and contained brick washboilers. Opening directly into this basement scullery was an apartment containing the water closet and a space for coal; it was completely underground, the ceiling of the apartment being the underside of the paving to the front path.

Steep, unlit stairs

Access to the basement was afforded by a winding staircase having poor headroom. Ceiling heights of the basements varied from 6ft. 5in. To 6ft. 8in. Other staircases were necessarily steep, winding and unlit. Halls and landings were extremely small where they existed, and resulted in a bewildering confliction of doors opening off them.

It will be readily understood that the central chimney serving six houses in each block was considerable interest. Though for simplification it has only been drawn into one block (B) on the sketch plan, it was repeated in all the others. The main flue within the stack followed the same shape as the building, i.e., hexagonal in plan. The outer face of the stack walls formed the back wall of the several rooms in the houses. Inside each house, this wall was of sufficient width to contain the normal firegate of the period.

Branch flues

The branch flue rose steeply above the grate and passed through the substantial thickness of brickwork of which the main stack was constructed, and joined the main flue in the direction of the flow.

In most blocks the central stack consisted of a single unobstructed flue on the lines of an industrial chimney; its internal diameter was about 2ft. 9 in. One stack, however, had an arrangement of mid-feathers forming separate flues to each house. As might be imagined "down-draught" troubles were not exactly unknown, but the general efficiency of the flues was much higher than one might expect. The upper opening of the stack was not protected in any way.

During demolition, it was revealed that efforts had been made to improve the performance of some of the firegates – drainpipes had been installed to form short vertical extensions of the branch flues within the main flue.

A further extraordinary device in the construction of the central stack was the incorporation of air-shafts to provide ventilation to the several houses. Each house had its own shafts, which were constructed vertically in the thickness of brickwork forming the main chimney. One shaft served each floor; hence in two-storey blocks, twelve shafts were encased in the brickwork (which averaged about 4ft. in thickness). The stacks to three-storey blocks thus contained a total of 18 of these ventilating ducts, which were cement-rendered throughout Within the houses, an air-brick on the wall at ceiling level communicated with the ventilating shaft and the duct was also extended downwards to a grille installed for the full width of the grate underneath the mantel. The upper end of the ventilation shafts finished either as air-bricks in the face of the stack above roof level or as apertures below corbelling courses. If these ducts served no other purpose, at least they precluded any suggestion that the houses had no through-ventilation!

The demolition of these houses marks the end of an unusual experiment. No one locally seems to know what led to it. A striving for density cannot have been the reason for the choice of design; working-class tenements had been built in the neighbouring town of Birkenhead 30 years previously, and the first municipal flats in Liverpool five years before the "concertina cottages" were planned. In any case, an equal or greater number of terraced houses could have been built on the site.

Economy of construction, especially of roofs and brickwork, has been suggested as the probable reason for the hexagonal pattern, but when the central chimney is examined, this explanation is not fully convincing. Maybe the design was merely an effort at "community development" long before the town-planners thought of it and was, in some respects, ahead of its time.

It only remains to add that an objection was lodged against making a clearance order for these houses. On behalf of the owner it was represented that only the basement-type blocks were so unfit as to require demolition or closure, and the remainder should be allowed to stand for a further five years. At the local inquiry, however, the owner withdrew his objection, but suggested that demolition of the blocks joined to the front houses should not be insisted upon, because of the difficulties which would arise in splitting the building along the line of the common chimney flues.

The clearance order was confirmed by the Minister without modification.

SEACOMBE SHIPYARDS

Shipyards came to Seacombe for a short time with the building of the docks in Wallasey Pool, just over 150 years ago. They were centred along the river front south of the ferry to Alfred Dock entrance. The first shipbuilders were Bowdler & Chaffer who were established in 1864. They were close to Seacombe Ferry and had a frontage of 250 feet with three slipways. In their first year of operation Bowdler & Chaffer built a landing stage for New Ferry and launched four ships. They built up a flourishing business and made a great name, supplying vessels to many famous Liverpool ship-owners. The best of the Seacombe-built boats was the yacht 'Sunbeam'. She was built for Lord Brassey and sailed the world. The business only lasted a short time and closed in 1877 after a serious fire on 31st January 1872 and a shipwright strike.

Other shipbuilders opened on the frontage. They included Andrews and Company who opened in 1865 but after building three vessels it closed a year later. Others included Thomas Vernon's & Sons, Alexander Jack and J,F, Waddington & Co. Vernon's opened in 1865 and closed four years later. Alexander Jack opened a yard in 1883 and it occupied 44,000 square yards. He spent £20,000 fitting it out. After building two vessels the yard went bankrupt and closed soon after.

Worthy of note is the last of the Seacombe Shipyards was Waddington's. In June, 1866, they took over from the yard vacated by Andrews and Company. James Waddington was indeed a man ahead of his time. He designed and built a submarine – or rather, a vessel something like one. He called it the 'Porpoise' and though the boat performed well in trials he failed to persuade the Royal Navy to take any notice. The craft was anchored off Seacombe for two years before finally being broken up. Waddington went bankrupt in 1887 and so ending a chapter of Seacombe shipyards. Big yards of other places killed them off.

LOOKING AT OLD VICTORIA ROAD

Borough Road, 1870

Borough Road was once known as Victoria Road. To help prevent any confusion with the Victoria Road of New Brighton the fire brigade asked for the road to be renamed and was duly done so in 1918.

Borough Road was one of the original roads of Poulton-cum-Seacombe, and became the main shopping area until Liscard was built up between both World Wars. The shops were the life line for many locals - before we had supermarkets. Scotts, Liversidge and Guests sold meat; Wilsons, Morrows and Herrons sold fruit and veg. Edward Brick sold and repair shoes. Everything you would find moreorless in a modern supermarket but all in one road. The major difference being there was more of a community feeling. Shopkeepers knew their customers and vice versa.

Borough Road, 1904

On the corner of Borough Road and Church Road was J.H.Scott, butchers. They opened in the 1890's and served the local community for more than 30 years before closing between the World Wars. Inside the butchers were large sides of beef hanging from hooks. The butcher would keep his shop clean with fresh sawdust on the floor and shining tiles on the walls. It was not unusual for housewives to buy bones to flavour their soups. Lumps of fat were on sale too for rendering down for dripping, which was a popular meal on its own, spread on a slice of toast. It was always beef dripping. It was commonplace to hang meat outside the shop.

TELEPHONE No. 17.   **TELEPHONE No. 17.**

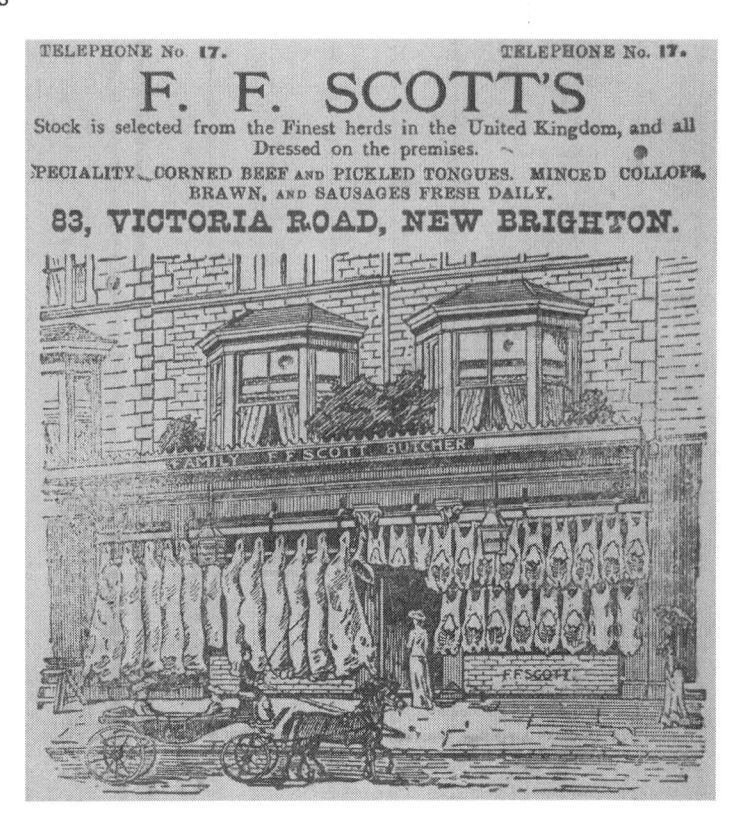

F. F. SCOTT'S

Stock is selected from the Finest herds in the United Kingdom, and all Dressed on the premises.

SPECIALITY — CORNED BEEF AND PICKLED TONGUES. MINCED COLLOPS, BRAWN, AND SAUSAGES FRESH DAILY.

83, VICTORIA ROAD, NEW BRIGHTON.

Off Borough Road was the large and charming house of Dr. Isaac Byerley. He was the 1st Poor Law Medical Officer for Health in Wallasey in 1873. The house he lived in was called Myrtle Cottage which was enclosed in a high wall and had a good fruit garden in which many pear and apple trees grew. When Byerley Street was built in the 1870's it was named after him. The cottage itself was demolished in the 1880's when Jubilee Grove was built – to coincide with Queen Victoria's 50 years on the throne in 1887.

THE IRVING THEATRE

Before the Irving Theatre on Borough Road was built there was a charming house. It was set back from the road and was called 'Hope House'. it was built in the 1860's and was occupied at first by Samuel Wright who was the Secretary and Manager of the West India & Pacific Steam Navigation Company.

By about 1867 the house was purchased by a turtle merchant, George Hulse. He was one of the biggest importers of turtles in Great Britain. There was a great demand for turtle soup which appeared in many restaurants. George had a shop in Dale Street, Liverpool, which had a large water tank full of live turtles swimming about. George died in 1870 and is buried in St. Hilary's Churchyard.

Posing for the camera on the grounds of Hope House is Mrs. Ann Hulse, her son John Edwin Hulse and grand-daughter

----

Various tenants lived at Hope House over the years including George's widow, Anne. By 1897 the house was bought by James Kiernan who set about demolishing the property and by 1899 had opened a theatre on the former site and gardens. Originally James wanted to build his new theatre where the Town Hall stands today. Much of the stone work for the new theatre came from St. George's Church, Lord Street, Liverpool, which was in the process of being demolished. The corner stone was laid on Wednesday, 11th October 1899 by Sir Henry Irving. Many were in attendance including his good friend Bram Stoker, the author of Dracula. The new theatre officially opened on 18th December 1899. Sir Henry allowed his name to be associated with the theatre on the strict understanding that the best of original drama would be produced there. Over the years the theatre was to go through various owners and different names - La Scala, Casino, Hippodrome and finally the Embassy before closing in 1936 after poor attendances. A year later the theatre re-opened as a cinema under the name Embassy again but closed in 1959 owing to lack of support. The building carried on for a time as a bingo establishment.

A DECADE OF CHANGE

View from the top of newly constructed Mersey Court. On the left is the bottom corner of Borough Road and in the distance is the Town Hall, 1963

So much of old Seacombe came tumbling down in the 1960's. Demolition men with bulldozers and large hammers knocked away so much to make way for the new tunnel approach or to erect new flats and maisonettes.
Clearance Orders swept away old streets, houses and shops off the map at the south end of the town. The face of Seacombe changed forever. Rubble strewn sites where familiar landmarks. Staring at skeletons of buildings.
Many houses in Seacombe had outside toilets, some had no bathrooms. Changes were needed. In 1961 Mersey Street made way for the towering 16-storey high 'Mersey Court' flats. Abbotsford

Street and Fell Street were next to be demolished. Maisonettes took their place. The former site of Seacombe Station was demolished and flats erected on the site.

Brighton Street, 1963. The municipal offices, South Annexe, now occupies the site.

By 1963 Brighton Street was next for development. Properties 108-116 were demolished to make way for the South Annexe municipal offices. The General Health Committee had indicated that the dwelling houses in the area were 'unfit for habitation or were by reason of their bad arrangement or the narrowness of the streets, dangerous or injurious to the health of the inhabitants of the area, and that the other buildings, if any, in the area were for a like reason dangerous and injurious to the health of inhabitants'.

In the same year more houses were demolished in Beaconsfield Road, Servia Street, Bosnia Street, Little Street, Smithy Lane, Tabor Street, Ellis Street, Shaw Street and many more streets. All demolished to make way for improved developments.

The following year saw more of Brighton Street demolished under Compulsory Purchase Orders. Small houses and small shops all crumpled to a heap of bricks and broken plaster. The whole of the right hand side of Brighton Street from its junction with Ellis Street came under the hammer.

Beaconfield Road demolition site, 1963

Many shops were empty. The death sentence on the properties was announced in 1962. Some shopkeepers lingered on as long as they could. The last of these was Jim Savage who ran a sweets and tobacconist's at the start of the doomed blocks. He had another shop in St. Paul's Road.

"Everyone round here has known for a long time that the places were coming down", said Jim to the Wallasey News, "and I think most people are now rather glad that something is really being done. The uncertainty has been worrying for us all".

Chemist Frank Mellows came to Number 24 Brighton Street, on the corner of Tabor Street, over thirty years before (as shown overleaf). He closed his shop in May 1964. "It's a wrench having to go", he said at the time, "but I suppose it has to be. Thirty years in the one place is a long time and we have made a lot of friends. It's been most touching this last week or so, having so many old customers and friends coming in to say goodbye. You make a lot of friends as a chemist. You get to know whole families. The old Post Office a few doors away closed early in the year. Most of the other businesses have ceased. It has been a bit of a ghost area. We have just been waiting for the inevitable".

The sound of breaking glass and collapsing walls saw the chemist and the post office as well as a funeral parlour and other little premises all gone. A roar as they fall, A great cloud of dust.

In 1966 the Council applied for Compulsory Purchase Orders for the demolition of Platt Street, Beatrice Street, and Leopold Street area. Only the latter surviving in name whilst the others were wiped off the map.

The building of the second Mersey Tunnel was authorised by the Mersey Tunnel Act, 1965, which received Royal Assent later in August. On 12th January, 1966, work began on sinking a 90 foot deep shaft with a ceremony taking place in Tudor Avenue. The ventilation shaft would see parts of Denman Grove and Tudor Avenue demolished as well as the properties on the promenade facing the river.

The building of the second Mersey Tunnel was authorised by the Mersey Tunnel Act, 1965, which received Royal Assent later in August. On 12th January, 1966, work began on sinking a 90 foot deep shaft with a ceremony taking place in Tudor Avenue. The ventilation shaft would see parts of Denman Grove and Tudor Avenue demolished as well as the properties on the promenade facing the river.

Start of the construction of the second Mersey Tunnel, a 90 foot deep shaft, at Tudor Avenue, 1966

The residents had to endure the dirt and din of the demolition and the noise of the heavy lorries.

Residing at Number 13 Tudor Avenue was Jean Miller who lived with her husband and teenager son. She told the Wallasey News journalist at the time as she watched the workings on the ventilation shaft. "We haven't been told anything officially. Some say we will be down within two to three years but meanwhile we must learn to live with a big workings at the bottom of the road. Children think that our houses have also been disposessed and throw stones at the windows. I have to leave the electric light burning all night".

At number 8 Tudor Avenue lived Mary Galvin, who had two small children and lived at the property for four years, said "We get all the dirt from the workings. It settles everywhere on the furniture and walls, even on the baby's clothes while they are airing. It will probably get worse once the houses are pulled down, as there will be dirt from the river. Of an evening we are plagued by children playing amongst the rubble of the demolished houses".

Tudor Avenue houses being demolished for the second Mersey Tunnel, 1966

By 1967 the second tunnel was to see other properties come tumbling down– as far as Wheatland Lane. Houses along the old railway line to Seacombe made way for road widening.

One of those properties was Reg Denton's long established shoe shop which was on the corner of Wheatland Lane. He set up his business after his army service in World War One. He said to the Wallasey News, "It's all in the name of progress, and demolition had to come, but I'm sorry to be going. I've been here a very long time and made a lot of good friends. I'm going to miss the shop, the people, and this part of Seacombe."

The last of the big changes was in 1972 with the demolition of the oldest houses in Seacombe – four acres that was bordered by Oakdale Road, Byron Road and Wheatland Lane. The houses were built a century before and all suffered with damp.

View of changing Seacombe. New 16-storey tower]Mersey Court' and surrounding maisonettes, 1966

Empty buildings lay dilapidated and waste pieces of land scattered the area for years to come. The character of old Seacombe went under Compulsory Orders and the construction of the second Mersey Tunnel. Seacombe had changed.

On Thursday, 24th June 1971 the tunnel was opened in a ceremony by Queen Elizabeth II. The total cost of constructing the tunnel was £32,500,000. Families who lost their houses or shopkeepers who lost their livelihood would say the personal cost was higher.

The dotted line across the Mersey shows the direction of the second Mersey Tunnel. Part of the crane equipment can be seen jutting up over the promenade

ACKNOWLEDGEMENTS

E.C.Woods
P.C.Brown
Noel Smith
Merseyside Railway History Group
Ian and Marilyn Boumphrey
Ralph Rimmer
Dr. Richard A. Smye
Wallasey News.

Printed in Great Britain
by Amazon